Classic Comfort Foods

contents

Classic Tuna Noodle Casserole 4

Easy Chicken Pot Pie 6

Turkey and Stuffing Casserole 8

Broccoli Fish Bake 10

Chili & Rice 12

Beef and Brew Stew 14

Hearty Vegetarian Chili 16

Three Cheese Baked Ziti with Spinach 18

Lasagna Roll-Ups 20

Tortellini-Vegetable Toss 22

Pork Chop Skillet Dinner 24

Quick Skillet Chicken & Macaroni Parmesan 26

Beef Taco Skillet 28

Beef Teriyaki 30

Classic Tuna Noodle Casserole

Makes 4 servings

PREP TIME
10 minutes

BAKE TIME
25 minutes

1	can (10¾ ounces) Campbell's® Condensed Cream of Celery Soup (Regular *or* 98% Fat Free)
½	cup milk
1	cup cooked peas
2	tablespoons chopped pimientos
2	cans (about 6 ounces *each*) tuna, drained and flaked
2	cups hot cooked medium egg noodles
2	tablespoons dry bread crumbs
1	tablespoon butter, melted

1. Heat the oven to 400°F. Stir the soup, milk, peas, pimientos, tuna and noodles in a 1½-quart baking dish. Stir the bread crumbs and butter in a small bowl.

2. Bake for 20 minutes or until the tuna mixture is hot and bubbling. Stir the tuna mixture. Sprinkle with the bread crumb mixture.

3. Bake for 5 minutes or until the bread crumbs are golden brown.

Kitchen Tips

Substitute Campbell's® Condensed Cream of Mushroom Soup for the Cream of Celery.

To melt the butter, remove the wrapper and place the butter in a microwavable cup. Cover and microwave on HIGH for 30 seconds.

CLASSIC COMFORT FOODS

CLASSIC COMFORT FOODS

Easy Chicken Pot Pie

Makes 4 servings

PREP TIME
10 minutes

BAKE TIME
30 minutes

1 can (10¾ ounces) Campbell's® Condensed Cream of Chicken Soup (Regular *or* 98% Fat Free)
1 package (about 9 ounces) frozen mixed vegetables, thawed
1 cup cubed cooked chicken *or* turkey
½ cup milk
1 egg
1 cup all-purpose baking mix

1. Heat the oven to 400°F. Stir the soup, vegetables and chicken in a 9-inch pie plate.

2. Stir the milk, egg and baking mix in a small bowl. Spread the batter over the chicken mixture.

3. Bake for 30 minutes or until the topping is golden brown.

Kitchen Tip

You can easily substitute Campbell's® Condensed Cream of Chicken with Herbs Soup for the Cream of Chicken.

CLASSIC COMFORT FOODS

Turkey and Stuffing Casserole

Makes 6 servings

PREP TIME
15 minutes

BAKE TIME
25 minutes

Vegetable cooking spray
1 can (10¾ ounces) Campbell's® Condensed Cream of Mushroom Soup (Regular *or* 98% Fat Free)
1 cup milk *or* water
1 bag (16 ounces) frozen vegetable combination (broccoli, cauliflower, carrots), thawed
2 cups cubed cooked turkey *or* chicken
4 cups Pepperidge Farm® Herb Seasoned Stuffing
1 cup shredded Swiss *or* Cheddar cheese (about 4 ounces)

Kitchen Tip

Substitute 3 cans (4.5 ounces each) Swanson® Premium White Chunk Chicken Breast in Water, drained, for the cubed cooked turkey.

1. Heat the oven to 400°F. Spray a 2-quart casserole with the cooking spray.

2. Stir the soup and milk in a large bowl. Add the vegetables, turkey and stuffing and mix lightly. Spoon the turkey mixture into the casserole.

3. Bake for 20 minutes or until the turkey mixture is hot and bubbling. Stir the turkey mixture. Top with the cheese.

4. Bake for 5 minutes or until the cheese is melted.

CLASSIC COMFORT FOODS

Broccoli Fish Bake

Makes 4 servings

PREP TIME
15 minutes

BAKE TIME
20 minutes

1 package (about 10 ounces) frozen broccoli spears, cooked and drained

4 fresh *or* thawed frozen firm white fish fillets (cod, haddock *or* halibut) (about 1 pound)

1 can (10¾ ounces) Campbell's® Condensed Cream of Broccoli Soup

⅓ cup milk

¼ cup shredded Cheddar cheese

2 tablespoons dry bread crumbs

1 teaspoon butter, melted

⅛ teaspoon paprika

Kitchen Tip

You can substitute 1 pound fresh broccoli spears, cooked and drained, for the frozen.

1. Place the broccoli into a 2-quart shallow baking dish. Top with the fish. Stir the soup and milk in a small bowl. Pour the soup mixture over the fish. Sprinkle with the cheese.

2. Stir the bread crumbs, butter and paprika in a small bowl. Sprinkle the crumb mixture over all.

3. Bake at 450°F. for 20 minutes or until the fish flakes easily when tested with a fork.

CLASSIC COMFORT FOODS

Chili & Rice

Makes 4 servings

PREP TIME
10 minutes

COOK TIME
25 minutes

- ¾ pound ground beef (85% lean)
- 1 medium onion, chopped (about ½ cup)
- 1 tablespoon chili powder
- 1 can (10¾ ounces) Campbell's® Healthy Request® Condensed Tomato Soup
- ¼ cup water
- 1 teaspoon vinegar
- 1 can (about 15 ounces) kidney beans, rinsed and drained
- 4 cups hot cooked regular long-grain white rice, cooked without salt

Kitchen Tip

This dish is delicious served topped with shredded reduced-fat Cheddar cheese.

1. Cook the beef, onion and chili powder in a 10-inch skillet over medium-high heat until the beef is well browned, stirring often. Pour off any fat.

2. Stir the soup, water, vinegar and beans in the skillet and heat to a boil. Reduce the heat to low. Cook for 10 minutes or until the mixture is hot and bubbling. Serve the beef mixture over the rice.

CLASSIC COMFORT FOODS

Beef and Brew Stew

Makes 8 servings

PREP TIME
20 minutes

COOK TIME
40 minutes

BAKE TIME
2 hours

3	tablespoons vegetable oil
3	pounds boneless beef chuck roast, cut into 1-inch pieces
2	large onions, sliced (about 2 cups)
2	cloves garlic, minced
2	cans (10¾ ounces *each*) Campbell's® Condensed Golden Mushroom Soup
2	cans (10½ ounces *each*) Campbell's® Condensed French Onion Soup
1	bottle (12 fluid ounces) dark beer *or* stout
1	tablespoon packed brown sugar
1	tablespoon cider vinegar
½	teaspoon dried thyme leaves, crushed
1	bay leaf
2	cups fresh *or* frozen whole baby carrots
	Egg noodles, cooked, drained and buttered

1. Heat **1 tablespoon oil** in an oven-safe 6-quart saucepot over medium-high heat. Add the beef in 3 batches and cook until well browned, stirring often, adding an additional **1 tablespoon** oil as needed during cooking. Remove the beef from the saucepot. Pour off any fat.

2. Heat the remaining oil in the saucepot over medium heat. Add the onions and garlic and cook until the onions are tender.

3. Stir the soups, beer, brown sugar, vinegar, thyme, bay leaf and carrots in the saucepot and heat to a boil. Cover the saucepot.

4. Bake at 300°F. for 2 hours or until the beef is fork-tender. Discard the bay leaf. Serve the beef mixture over the noodles.

CLASSIC COMFORT FOODS

CLASSIC COMFORT FOODS

Hearty Vegetarian Chili

Makes 4 servings

PREP TIME
10 minutes

COOK TIME
20 minutes

2	tablespoons vegetable oil
1	large onion, chopped (about 1 cup)
1	small green pepper, chopped (about ½ cup)
¼	teaspoon garlic powder *or* 2 small garlic cloves, minced
1	tablespoon chili powder
½	teaspoon ground cumin
2½	cups V8® 100% Vegetable Juice
1	can (about 15 ounces) black beans *or* red kidney beans, rinsed and drained
1	can (about 15 ounces) pinto beans, rinsed and drained

1. Heat the oil in a 2-quart saucepan over medium heat. Add the onion, green pepper, garlic powder, chili powder and cumin and cook until the vegetables are tender, stirring occasionally.

2. Stir the vegetable juice in the saucepan and heat to a boil. Reduce the heat to low. Cook for 5 minutes.

3. Stir in the beans and cook until the mixture is hot and bubbling.

CLASSIC COMFORT FOODS

Three Cheese Baked Ziti with Spinach

Makes 6 servings

PREP TIME
15 minutes

BAKE TIME
30 minutes

1	package (16 ounces) **uncooked** medium tube-shaped pasta (ziti)
1	bag (6 ounces) baby spinach, washed (about 4 cups)
1	jar (1 pound 9 ounces) Prego® Marinara Italian Sauce
1	cup ricotta cheese
4	ounces shredded mozzarella cheese (about 1 cup)
¾	cup grated Parmesan cheese
½	teaspoon garlic powder
¼	teaspoon ground black pepper

1. Prepare the pasta according to the package directions. Add the spinach during the last minute of the cooking time. Drain the pasta and spinach well in a colander. Return them to the saucepot.

2. Stir the Italian sauce, ricotta, ½ **cup** of the mozzarella cheese, ½ **cup** of the Parmesan cheese, garlic powder and black pepper into the pasta mixture. Spoon the pasta mixture into a 13×9×2-inch shallow baking dish. Sprinkle with the remaining mozzarella and Parmesan cheeses.

3. Bake at 350°F. for 30 minutes or until the mixture is hot and bubbling.

CLASSIC COMFORT FOODS

Lasagna Roll-Ups

Makes 4 servings

PREP TIME
30 minutes

BAKE TIME
35 minutes

STAND TIME
10 minutes

1 cup ricotta cheese

1 can (about 4 ounces) mushroom stems and pieces, drained

½ cup refrigerated pesto sauce

8 lasagna noodles, cooked and drained

2 cups Prego® Traditional Italian Sauce *or* Tomato, Basil & Garlic Italian Sauce

¾ cup Pace® Picante Sauce

4 ounces shredded mozzarella cheese (about 1 cup)

1. Stir the ricotta, mushrooms and pesto in a medium bowl. Top **each** noodle with ¼ **cup** of the cheese mixture. Spread to the edges. Roll up like a jelly roll. Place the rolls seam-side down in a 2-quart shallow baking dish.

2. Stir the Italian sauce and picante sauce in a small bowl and pour the mixture over the roll-ups.

3. Bake at 400°F. for 30 minutes or until they're hot and bubbling. Top with the mozzarella cheese. Bake for 5 minutes or until the cheese is melted. Let stand for 10 minutes.

CLASSIC COMFORT FOODS

CLASSIC COMFORT FOODS

Tortellini-Vegetable Toss

Makes 4 servings

PREP TIME
5 minutes

COOK TIME
15 minutes

1 jar (24 ounces) Prego® Chunky Garden Combination Italian Sauce

1 bag (16 ounces) frozen vegetable combination (broccoli, cauliflower, carrots)

1 package (16 ounces) frozen cheese-filled tortellini, cooked and drained

Grated Parmesan cheese

1. Heat the Italian sauce in a 3-quart saucepan over medium heat to a boil. Stir in the vegetables. Cover and cook for 10 minutes or until the vegetables are tender-crisp, stirring occasionally.

2. Put the tortellini in a large serving bowl. Pour the vegetable mixture over the tortellini. Toss to coat. Serve with the cheese.

CLASSIC COMFORT FOODS

Pork Chop Skillet Dinner

Makes 4 servings

PREP TIME
10 minutes

COOK TIME
40 minutes

1	tablespoon olive oil
4	bone-in pork chops, ¾-inch thick **each**
1	medium onion, chopped (about ½ cup)
1	cup *uncooked* regular long-grain white rice
1¼	cups Swanson® Chicken Stock
1	cup orange juice
3	tablespoons chopped fresh parsley
¼	teaspoon ground black pepper
4	orange slices

1. Heat the oil in a 12-inch skillet over medium-high heat. Add the pork and cook until well browned on both sides.

2. Add the onion and rice to the skillet. Cook until the rice is lightly browned.

3. Stir in the stock, orange juice, **2 tablespoons** parsley and black pepper and heat to a boil. Reduce the heat to low. Cover and cook for 20 minutes or until the pork is cooked through and the rice is tender. Top with the orange slices and sprinkle with the remaining parsley.

CLASSIC COMFORT FOODS

Quick Skillet Chicken & Macaroni Parmesan

Makes 6 servings

PREP TIME
15 minutes

COOK TIME
15 minutes

STAND TIME
5 minutes

- 1 jar (24 ounces) Prego® Traditional Italian Sauce *or* Tomato, Basil & Garlic Italian Sauce
- ¼ cup grated Parmesan cheese
- 1 can (12.5 ounces) Swanson® Premium White Chunk Chicken Breast in Water, drained
- 2 cups elbow pasta, cooked and drained (about 3 cups)
- 1 cup shredded mozzarella cheese (about 4 ounces)

1. Heat the Italian sauce, Parmesan cheese, chicken and pasta in a 10-inch skillet over medium-high heat to a boil. Reduce the heat to medium and cook for 10 minutes or until the mixture is hot and bubbling, stirring occasionally.

2. Sprinkle with the mozzarella cheese. Let stand for 5 minutes or until the cheese is melted.

CLASSIC COMFORT FOODS

Beef Taco Skillet

Makes 4 servings

PREP TIME
5 minutes

COOK TIME
20 minutes

- 1 pound ground beef
- 1 can (10¾ ounces) Campbell's® Condensed Tomato Soup (Regular *or* Healthy Request®)
- ½ cup Pace® Picante Sauce
- ½ cup water
- 6 flour tortillas (6-inch), cut into 1-inch pieces
- ½ cup shredded Cheddar cheese

1. Cook the beef in a 10-inch skillet over medium-high heat until well browned, stirring often to separate the meat. Pour off any fat.

2. Stir the soup, picante sauce, water and tortillas in the skillet and heat to a boil. Reduce the heat to low. Cook for 5 minutes. Stir the beef mixture. Top with the cheese.

Creamy Mexican Fiesta: Stir in ½ **cup** sour cream with the soup.

Ranchero Style: Use corn tortillas instead of flour tortillas and shredded Mexican cheese blend instead of Cheddar.

CLASSIC COMFORT FOODS

Beef Teriyaki

Makes 4 servings

PREP TIME
10 minutes

COOK TIME
15 minutes

- 2 tablespoons cornstarch
- 1¾ cups Swanson® Beef Stock
- 2 tablespoons soy sauce
- 1 tablespoon packed brown sugar
- ½ teaspoon garlic powder
- 1 boneless beef sirloin steak
- 4 cups fresh *or* frozen broccoli florets
- Hot cooked rice

1. Stir the cornstarch, stock, soy sauce, brown sugar and garlic powder in a small bowl until the mixture is smooth.

2. Stir-fry the beef in a 10-inch nonstick skillet over medium-high heat until well browned, stirring often. Pour off any fat.

3. Add the broccoli to the skillet and cook for 1 minute. Stir in the cornstarch mixture. Cook and stir until the mixture boils and thickens. Serve the beef mixture over the rice.

Kitchen Tip

To make slicing easier, freeze the beef for 1 hour before slicing.

CLASSIC COMFORT FOODS